COMMISSIONS Y CORRIDOS

THE ALBUQUERQUE POET LAUREATE SERIES

Co-published with the City of Albuquerque's Department of Arts &
Culture, the Albuquerque Poet Laureate Series features new and selected
work by the city's Poet Laureate at the conclusion of their two-year term.
Newly appointed poets will join Hakim Bellamy, Jessica Helen Lopez,
Manuel González, Michelle Otero, and Mary Oishi as significant voices
in the community who have been recognized with the honor of serving
as the Poet Laureate and sharing their craft in the volumes published in
the series.

Also available in The Albuquerque Poet Laureate Series:

The Blood Poems by Jessica Helen Lopez
Duende de Burque: Alburquerque Poems and Musings by Manuel González
Bosque: Poems by Michelle Otero

COMMISSIONS

CORRIDOS POEMS

HAKIM BELLAMY

UNIVERSITY OF NEW MEXICO PRESS

CITY OF ALBUQUERQUE DEPARTMENT OF ARTS & CULTURE

ALBUQUERQUE

ONE
ALBUQUE
RQUE

arts & culture

ISBN 978-0-8263-6317-6 (paper)
ISBN 978-0-8263-6318-3 (e-book)

Library of Congress Control Number: 2021937813

Founded in 1889, the University of New Mexico sits on the traditional homelands of the Pueblo of Sandia. The original peoples of New Mexico Pueblo, Navajo, and Apache since time immemorial have deep connections to the land and have made significant contributions to the broader community statewide. We honor the land itself and those who remain stewards of this land throughout the generations and also acknowledge our committed relationship to Indigenous peoples. We gratefully recognize our history.

Cover photograph: adapted from photograph by Kyle Johnson on Unsplash
Designed by Felicia Cedillos
Composed in Bembo Std 11/15

In honor of my father, Dr. Rev. Edward F. Bellamy.
This is why I had to be so far away, Dad. I miss you.
With gratitude to my mother, for my first book of poems.
Kaylem, you're my best poem.
Francesca and Max, I love you. Couldn't do this without you.
To my brothers and their families, I hope I make you
as proud as you make me.

CONTENTS

SERIES FOREWORD

As I write this introduction, it is April 2021, and Albuquerque has had Poets Laureate for nine years, beginning in April 2012. To date, five talented, unique, brilliant, and generous poets have been named Albuquerque Poet Laureate—each with a particular voice and a powerful story, each with a special connection to Albuquerque, both the place and the people.

Every two years the administration, selection, and public role of Albuquerque's Poet Laureate is the result of a unique and vibrant collaboration between the community-led Albuquerque Poet Laureate Program (APLP) and the Department of Arts & Culture for the City of Albuquerque. The APLP was established by poets and artists in 2010 to celebrate poetry by recognizing a resident poet who makes meaningful connections, honors and serves our diverse community, elevates the importance of the art form, and shares poetry with Albuquerque residents.

The APLP is coordinated by a seven-person organizing committee that is made up of poets and artists. The Poet Laureate is chosen biannually by a separate seven-person selection committee that represents the diversity of the Albuquerque community and the breadth of the poetry community. The APLP Organizing Committee supports the Selection Committee through a careful review of the competitive applications received and a consensus-based decision process to select an Albuquerque Poet Laureate.

The APLP announces the Poet Laureate with support from the City, and the Department of Arts & Culture coordinates and contracts with each Poet Laureate to implement a community project during their two-year tenure. The Poet Laureate writes occasional poems for the City and is often invited to participate in major City events. The APLP and Department of Arts & Culture both support the work and outreach of the current Poet Laureate in various ways.

Under the leadership of Mayor Tim Keller, the Department of Arts & Culture committed to sponsoring a book series celebrating each of the Poets Laureate, from the first Poet Laureate in 2012 through the present and into the future. We are grateful for the investment by and partnership with the University of New Mexico Press, which brought this series from a good idea to a beautiful reality. Albuquerque's impressive cohort of Poets Laureate has been writing with, for, and about Albuquerque for almost a decade, and we offer these bound gifts of words back to Albuquerque—the place and the people.

Shelle Sanchez, PhD
Director, Department of Arts & Culture
City of Albuquerque

PREFACE

This city is more than inspiring; it is a coauthor.

Let me explain. Sometimes poets laureate get to write poems for fun or necessity that are *not* occasional poems. The poems in this collection are not all commissions. And the poems are not corridos, per se. They are not eight quatrains that are four to six lines each. The lines are not octosyllabic. The rhythm is not duple meter. The music is inaudible. The corridista is Black.

But they *are* songs. They are songs about my life in this place, full of characters (including Burque itself) real and make believe. Helplessly mortal and hopeful, these songs are sometimes dreams and sometimes memories. Things I don't want to forget. Things I don't want *us* to forget. Things I want us to become.

Beyond providing a community with a sense of cultural identity and pride, a corrido offers an interpretation of certain well-known past events that should exist as common knowledge to the community. I offer this collection of poems, and my time as laureate, as an earnest attempt to accomplish this. That same desire is what marries the corridos in this collection to the commissions. As I mentioned, not all the poems collected here are commissions. Some were not even composed during my tenure as city laureate. That is by design, partially because when one's city ordains someone with the responsibility of capturing history as it evolves in real time, in verse, you never get to put it down.

However, it is also because my term was all of me. Not only did Albuquerque's decision to select me as the city's first poet laureate define me as an artist, it also (by virtue of its selection) made a profound statement that my experience as a thirty-four-year-old Black man in America was as New Mexican as different-colored chile. In a place where nothing is black'n white, where everything is Christmas, Albuquerque accepted my realism for magic.

When I am asked how long it takes me to write a poem, my answer is always a function of whatever age I am at the time of the poem request. At the time of this writing, I am forty-two years old. Therefore, by my math, it took me forty-two years to write this. It took all of me to write this, just as it took all of me to serve as poet laureate of this great city—a city that took a chance on me and put me on its shoulders and forever changed my life as a result. So as much as these poems are a thank you, they are all written after my induction ceremony because there is no going back, Albuquerque. We are inextricably bound from here on out, and everything I write is about you.

ONE HUNDRED YEARS OF CORRIDOS: A SONG FOR THE NEW MEXICO CENTENNIAL

In the first chapter
of the Gospel
according to Anaya
Rudolfo writes . . .

"All of the older people spoke only Spanish,
and I myself understood only Spanish . . ."

. . . in English.

¡Bienvenidos Albuquerque!
I myself understand only English

. . . in Diné.

We speak many languages
but mean the same thing,
and mañana will be more of the same.

Familia.
    Food.
        Fiesta.
            Forever.

(sung) *Come on and sing along!*
We're going to
Familia . . .
    Comida . . .
        Fiesta . . .
            Forever . . .
For one hundred years BC

before the Commodores
before Lionel Ritchie
and for a hundred years more
we've farmed, feasted, and fixed cars.

We've moved people
and mixed razas,
we've got an appointment with the curandera
as soon as we leave the doctor's.

A lust for livestock
like chupacabras.

Afraid of God
and the inexplicable . . .

¡Dinosaur fossils!

So in love with space
and the people who live there
that we speak Chewbacca.

The forty-seventh state
admitted to the Union,
we might as well have been the moon

. . . of Endor
to our forefathers.

With the oldest
and highest
state capital in the country,
people on both coasts
should look up to us
instead of wondering
if they have to exchange their money
before coming.

YES,

dollars is our official currency too,
and though
we don't have much of it
money can't buy cultura.

Our history book—
the King Alfonso version—
is a canon
of war and peace,

a Bible
of you and me

that was written in Madrid
by missionaries and mestizos.

We are men of magic
and women of wizardry
who speak in spell and song,

wing words
and fly them like a flag
all yellow
between red and green
like a traffic light,
like the state question is
hurry up
or slow down,

never stop.

All of the older people sung only corridos.
However, in those corridos.
Me? I only heard gospel.

Maybe it's me,
maybe it's a stage,

but every time
I hear the clap of thunder
it sounds like a blessing.

Every time
I hear the pitter-patter
of rain

it sounds
like a round
of applause,

and even the monsoon roars,
"Encore,"
as the flash bloods flood
our hearts with love.

One hundred New Year's Eves
of trying to puncture precipitation
where the sky never dies
and the clouds wear bulletproof vests
where we perpetually live

in the shadow of a hot-air balloon eclipse.

We are not a city
that speaks, "Good morning,"
we are a city that speaks
Mass Ascension,

Like Grandpa only spoke Spanish
while he was drinking.

Buenos Dias

Like Grandma only spoke Latin
when she was praying.

Buenas Noches

Where water
is so sacred and scarce
that we pot it in puddles
on our flat roofs,

pool it in vestibule
stoups of steepled temples
where pigeons swirl and roost,

pond it in mountaintops
on our not-so-flat horizons,

bottle it in our bodies
and then set fire to it in our forests.

Where it sounds like
acequias babble "amen"
and bosques smell like baptisms.

Where the rain
doesn't speak any language,
it only understands dance,

and sometimes

we miss it so much
we need TWO rainbows
to promise us it is coming back.

After thousands of years of owners
for this little piece of hacienda
it's been us as tenants

together,

roommates for the past hundred
call it a trust,
call it a Zia-shaped symbol for eternity
over our right ring finger,
call it the interconnectedness of cultures,
call it married to each other—
speak now or forever hold your "chisme."

We are
actions speak louder than wordsmiths,
storytelling rituals.

We don't speak Project Runway.
We cowboy cosmopolitan,
urban traditional.

Where our children dare not say or see
"Cucui" or "La llorona"
but are lucky Santa speaks Spanglish
and has a sweet tooth for leche y biscochitos.

Where birthdays are miracles
and each one has a spirit,
    Holy Spirit,
        or patron saint.

Where we celebrate one hundred

today.

In the beginning,
the Greatest Spirit
created America
    and the earth
        and it was

bueno.

I don't speak perfect English,
barely even speak passable Spanish,
but it's okay
because there is no such thing
as "perfect English"
except for the word

Nuevo Mexico.

NEW MEXICO DEPARTMENT OF TOURISM (A HAIKU)

Albuquerque. Where
the desert doesn't get in
the way of your view.

FISHER PRICE SCHOOL OF MEDICINE

Written for the Health Affairs's "Narrative Matters" Symposium

I

The last time I went to the doctor
I was eleven.

She was more pigtails than lab coat.
Her only qualification was a plastic
stethoscope. The glasses she wore
had no lenses. Not exactly an optometrist,
but her IQ was no stretch of the imagination.
She could see exactly what
was wrong with me, after just a handful
of questions. Diet, lifestyle, heartbreak,
heartbreak, heart . . .

She was elevator music.
I was slightly high blood pressure,
otherwise the picture of health.
She somehow knew that a smile
was the best kind of medicine,

so she gave me hers.
As I left, I took mine too,
and called her in the morning.

II

The next time I go to the doctor's,
I will have some questions for her.
I will ask her why every day I get out of bed
and feel less and less eleven.
Why my joints never ached in bad weather,
but now hollow every night at 5:30 and 6:00 p.m.
when the weatherman brings bad news.

I'll ask her if life is a death sentence,
if living is a terminal disease.
Sometimes this ride begins
and ends in an emergency room,
but it really starts and stops in between.

I'll ask her what happened to house visits.
Tell her all about how I've been sleeping,
over a cup of tea,
because the six-minute average
doctor-patient interaction
is not enough to "treat" me.

I will unpack my recurring nightmares
before her like a roadmap to my anxiety.
Take a handful of all those li'l pretty purple pills
that I refuse to let her prescribe me,
and connect the dots back to my historical trauma.

I will explain to her why every time I push and twist
the top off them drug store bottles it smells like cotton.
That it is not her job to childproof me from my past,
that there aren't enough milligrams in that script
to rewrite it or fix it, her job ain't even to help me live with it.
Her job is to help me outlive it.

Then, I will pour her another cup, because I am not done.

I will ask her to explain me the difference
between healthcare and "who cares."
I will ask her what it will take
to incentivize death prevention?

I will suggest
that if the measure of a health professional
is how many lives they save,

why wait till we roll into the examination room sideways
when it should profit her to protect us
while we are still standing up?

Will we wait
until more black boys die at the hands of police
than diabetes to consider violence
an institutional health issue?

Will we wait
until our children put two and two together;
do the math, the science,
the English and the Social Studies
only to remind us, every few months or so,
that broken school plus broken homes
means the game is fixed?

Will we wait
'til Mother Nature is in hospice,
her immune system thin as ozone,
her polar caps bald as chemo,
to reconsider what "World Health Organization"
aught to mean?

When will we start saving lives outside?

. . . and she will be waiting,
for me to finally stop asking questions.
And I will tell her,
we've been waiting to death,
like patients,
when we are wanting to be fed,
like pupils with the potential to bloom.

The next time I see her,
I will tell her there's no need to wash her hands.

The dirtier, the better.
Leave your sleeves rolled up.

We need more than a surgeon general—
we need a pediatric infantry.
A frontline of physicians
slingin' arms into armistices,
instead of armor and stitches.

Because I'm no PhD,
but it stands to reason that war
is pretty much the most unhealthy thing we do to ourselves,
next to not brushing our teeth.
It's more than a cavity in the ground,
it's a cavity of the soul, and I know
what she'll say . . .

"Dammit, Jim,
I'm not a pastor."

However, unlike a priest
you aren't just there at dusk
to hold hands, close eyelids,
and console us.

You are also there at dawn,
the first sight for sore eyes,
and if we're lucky, even a smack on the behind
to comfort us.

And I just wish
I saw you a few more Sundays in between.
Because there's so much healing to do
that I don't wanna wait till I'm hurt
to see a doctor.

III

The last time I ever go see a doctor,
I will ask her
what took her so long.

I'll wonder,
after this many years
and that many smarts,
how in heaven
she still hasn't found
a vaccine for broken hearts

or a way to add padding
to the walls of my father's brain
so his memories can't escape.

I'll tell her my worst dreams
of high school cafeterias
with semiautomatic handguns
in vending machines.

I'll suggest
that there is no such thing
as a "mental-health day"
in a world so chemically imbalanced,
biological warfare is in our bloodstream.
It's more like a staycation
in a hospital or a holding cell,
incarcerated in our membranes,
and retail therapy is a grossly inadequate cure.

I'll ask her if I'll live,
and she won't make any promises
or percentages.

She won't even order an X-Ray or an MRI,
because she's got the same magic glassless glasses
she's had since she was nine.
She already knows what's inside.

Her laugh will have the same
effect it did on my blood pressure when I was eleven.

She'll tell me I'm not crazy,
just a hypochondriac.
That we're all dying daily,
and some of us are just waiting,
better or worse,
slower and faster
than others.

She'll give me a smile
and tell me it's contagious,
then send me back out into this ecosystem
of people smoking on treadmills
and jogging into the smog.

But at least she'll call
and practice the forgotten art
of "checking on me tomorrow."
And when I ask her, again,
if I'll live,

she'll tell me the truth.
She'll say, "No,
but you'll be okay."

BLESS ME

Inspired by the life and literature of Rudolfo Anaya

No, Antonio.
You are not broken.

You will fix us
in the places
that miracles have failed
and forgotten.

Eastern New Mexico
has been fighting
long before World War II,

and it's quite normal
for war
to make people lose their faith . . .

in everything.

But you
are fact,
and where you are from
is fertile.

Here,
they harvest soldiers
and priests
for lunch.

But you are cosmic.
A constellation of culture
that could tip the entire
llano toward the sun

just to get her attention.
To remind her
that we are her children,
dying to get closer to her
by bullet or belief.

And you, Antonio,
will concern yourself
with the fate of every soul,
while the church concerns itself
with the fate
of every pocket.

Guadalupe is more than just your home, Antonio.
It is where your heart is buried
beneath the beaten,
beneath the beatings,
beneath your classmates mocking you,
"Bless me, Antonio!"
Beneath the beating earth pumping mud through our veins.

I may be no virgin,
but as sure as Juan Diego
smelled the rose petals on Our Lady's breath,
I will give you this Nahua,

this language of healing
and curanderismo,
in hopes that you one day find yourself, Antonio.

And when you do,
perhaps
you will find your God
curled up behind you.

Protect him.
Speak to him
in the tongue of the land I taught you.

Then,
tell him to pick up a shovel
and saddle up!

Because there are too many miracles
and not enough time.

Because this is the army
the priests should have prayed for,
the army soldiers should have joined.

Because we need
all the help
we can get.

In the year of our Constitution 1787, our country was already over 150 years into the practice of creating FREE & CHEAP laborers for life. And in 1786, printers in our then capital of Philadelphia conducted the first successful strike for increased wages.

Over a hundred years later, in 1902, a former dressmaker and schoolteacher known simply as Mother Jones would be called "the most dangerous woman in America."

And over a hundred years to now, we still have a long way to go in a country that democratically elects leaders who genuinely believe that underpaid teachers (& their unions) are the biggest threat to our future.

—HB

BREAD & ROSES

after Helen Todd and James Oppenheim

The very first unions in America
were brought here by boat,
broken by back.

By whip,
rape,
and rope.

Nowadays,
lies
and a bogeyman economy
do the trick.

The only thing scarier
than labor
is losing it.

Even the House
and Senate
can come together
around house
and field.

Divide and conquer.

Give us power
but not position.
Give us personnel
but not privilege.
Give us responsibility
but not rights
nor profits
nor shares.

Give us a sniff
of American exceptionalism.
Get us drunk
off of upward mobility.

Put us behind the wheel
of the American Dream
until we launch ourselves
into a windshield
that will not let us eject
or escape
this cabin.

I come from
a long line of laborers,

a lineage of long Black men

who nowadays
only unionize for sport,
who are either
rich enough to be locked out
or poor enough
to be locked in,

but back then
were Memphis enough
to get Dr. King
to detour toward death
in the name of fairness.

Air Jordan-esque working conditions.
Laceless wages.
Boots
that were begging for straps.

We are colonial Philadelphia.
1806ers.
Journeymen
convicted of criminal conspiracy.

We are New York 1829.
Workingmen's Party.

When sixty hours and
a six-day workweek
was radical.

Every morning
we wake up Knights of Labor
to whistles of work
and whispers of worse.

Integrated women
and our own Negro spirituals of sorts
hold the forts.

At a time when mining companies
would send dynamite husbands
home in a bucket,

and mothers,
like Jones,
who lived in homes
rented from the employer,
fed family
with currency
only good at the company store.

Who had three days
to replace "Papa"
with one of her sons
so production doesn't suffer.

No matter how young we was.
No matter how much she does.

We are immigrants, Mollies.
1877 pushed too far.
We are the children
worked too hard.

The reason Mary Harris marched
from the City of Brotherly Love
to Teddy Roosevelt's front porch.

We found our own Congress
of Industrial Organizations
to replace the one
that had forsaken us.

We are sit-down strikes
in the buildings they value
with our bodies
that they do not.

We are wage equity
and wage war.

We are ripped-off scabs
that will not bandage their cuts after we strike,

only band together
our blood
and heal.

We are still leaping
from ninth-floor windows
at the Triangle Waist Company.

We are Clara Lemlich.
We are Delores Huerta.
We are Cesar Chavez.
We are Samuel Gompers.
We are Gabriel Prosser.
We are Lucy Gonzalez Parson.
And we are Rosie the Riveter.

We are the hand on the Bible
denying we're socialist.
We are the witches of Taft-Hartley.

We are holy, Jerry Fallwell!

Salt of the Earth
who forever put love of God
before love of Greed.

You said,

"Labor unions should study and read the Bible
instead of asking for more money . . ."

But we are pickers
who reap and sow
and read.

Sirach 34:22:
"To take away a neighbor's living
is to murder him; to deprive an employee of his wage
is to shed blood."

We are teamsters and longshoremen,
and just like you
we ain't perfect.

Proverbs 14:31:
"He who oppresses a poor man,
insults his Maker."

We are closed factories
and empty mouths.
Auto, textiles, and steel.

We are the meek
who inherit ourselves.
We are the lamb,
the sacrifice, and the carpenter
that said:

"The worker deserves his wages."
—Luke 10:7

We are the people
who power dreams
and profit.

And are for granted.
And are forgotten.

We are the people who brought you the weekend.
We aren't coming home empty-handed.
We are back pockets of college tuition.
We are stuffed between the mattresses of future Christmases.

We are smiles
on our children's faces,
and even though we are sometimes faceless
we are food in the fridge.

We are hero and heroine.
We are coming back.
            Coming home.
                        Every night.
In one piece.

Please, *please* believe
that we are all hard work
and belief.

We are about 5:05

                5:30

            6:15

We
are bread and roses
for dinner.

BLUE CORN SPECIAL

there is butter in the barrio
that will not let us slide

or slip
in la cocina

we will take a kitchen to our worries like sugarcane
weed people out of our lives
like . . . weeds

put butt
on back
meat on bone and
too-skinny nephews

. . . like butter

put family in marrow
like oso buco
put family in morrow
like leftovers

there is butter in the barrio
that will not let us lose weight
that keeps us afflicted
with heavy heart disease
like we've got a crush on ourselves

because our capacity for love
is bigger than our waist lines

because we will fit a feast day
and a pheasant
in the center of a circle of friends
like an open mouth
waiting for rain

we wear our dinner
like blackberry rouge
a swollen jaw full of seconds
always coming back for more

Home cooked and half-baked
we eat hella good
even when hell is bad
we stand in the heat
we live in the kitchen

comfort food
'til we're uncomfortable

we smile huge
with our hips
from cheek to cheek
stuffing "I don't care" in our right pocket
and stuffing "I don't cholesterol"
in our left

we are a buffalo buffet
no bull

there is butter in the barrio
that will not let us burn

just brown

fly like tortilla
never drown
not even at the cantina
as sure as fry bread floats

cheat charity with chicharrones
cash poor
but abundant in familia
a surplus of sisters
and the myriad of dishes we can whip up
from corn, bean & squash

we put the carne in carnale
flesh of my flesh
blood of my . . .

tofu?

we are as green as the farmer
and as red as his boots

we sound like my uncle
when I was young and chunky
and he said I was on a seafood diet
cause when you don't know when your next meal is coming
you eat all the food you see

we sound like my father
when his son left for college a carnivore
and came back eating only leaves
and he said, "Son,
tummy doesn't grow on trees"

we sound like a good conversation
the perfect pair to every meal
like laughter
and it doesn't matter
white or red

put our values where our mouth is
like we're vegans

we are all eyes
bigger than stomachs that go down swinging

by mortar and pestle
we make masa of the mesa
as it rolls itself thin as the horizon is yellow
toward the blue corn sky

there is butter in the barrio
that should have killed us by now
but in the belly of the beast
you gotta try harder than that

we will feed a multitude with five bushels of red
and two fish
. . . as long as you don't ask where the fish comes from

when life gave us limes
we made tequila
and a mean lime-butter sauce
that really brings a dish together . . .

like people

we are like butter, baby

we are the butter in the barrio
that has fueled warriors
and fertilized wombs

slathered blankets of our hands
over beds of flour
and yielded a sea of sopapilla

we are whom we eat

as we snap
crackle
dance
and sing

in this comal of a desert
that gives us life
one meal at a time

FOR "NIKKI"

I
I feel like you've always been mine
though you've been proclaiming emancipation since before
since before we was slave or citizen
since we was love and laughter and light
we don't own each other no mo'
some stopped saving one another too

but you
have turned borders into water
language into papers

death into understanding
and day-to-day into magic

does being a sHE-RO ever get old?
or just old-fashioned?

II
Some people want to be like you when they grow up
I want to be like you NOW
Edward, son of Edward Frederick, they call me Hakim
Yolande Cornelia Jr.
they call you Nikki

third sign of the Zodiac
they call us talkers

we come from East Coast and Appalachia
Philadelphia to Tennessee and Black

back and forth
blonde and 'fro

we come from Black People
Black Churches and Black-Eyed Peas, sista

poets and not quite poets
if you ask Ivory Tower
instead of Ivory Coast,
but who asked them anyway?

for the record,
I too, prefer my wine . . . red

III
When I heard the news
I thought of you

I had a few friends that went to Virginia Tech
none at that time
at that time
you were the only person I knew, but did not know
that went there

I think about the sanctuary of the sentence
where we sometimes hide
sometimes say come and get me
I think about how schoolhouses
ain't never been safe in the South
I think about how everywhere is the South

and though hip hop is the new underground
your words have always been a railroad

WE ARE VIRGINIA TECH

IV
Do you ever get tired of fighting fire with paper?
this many books in,

do you still feel like people misread you?
will you figure out a way
to bottle "relevance" and sell it to the next generation of Giovannis?
will you blueprint your survival of America,
cancer and Black womanhood . . .

or is it already embedded in the hieroglyphs
of your "codexes"

do your codices, code exist?
how do you commit our existence to script
with such vivid depiction?

and I know you been chasing her
like an old game of tag
maybe even laid an index finger on her once

or twice

but next time you get close enough to Utopia
close enough to smell her hair
you tell her I am looking for her . . . please

V
They will call you distinguished, Professor,
activist, human or civil

they will call you an American writer
or an African American writer

a great poet
or a great Black poet

never both
when you are both
and more

but a wise person once said,
"Once you know who you are,
you don't have to worry anymore."

DOC: A MONOLOGUE TRYPTYCH

Doc:
I first saw Mr. Ray
as my patient
in Los Angeles
January 1968

he'd seen a scientologist
a hypnotist
and now he was in my chair

had a family history of mental patients
son of a prostitute
and a father who had been in and out of jail

grocery stores
paycheck stores
taxi cabs and office buildings
Ray was a robber, stick-up artist

learned to shoot
in the Army
but didn't learn much else
discharged for ineptness and lack of ability
his military record said
he chafed at authority
was drunk, AWOL
didn't follow orders very well

I suspect he suffered from a learning disorder
his school records
reveal him as an outcast among his peers
the teachers actually wrote

that they found him "repulsive"
and "aggressive"

Mr. Ray failed the first grade
now, I certainly would not say this in earshot of my client
but he certainly was not the brightest bulb in the bunch
no one would call him brilliant
but it'd be a mistake to call him dumb

there was evidence of a dissociative disorder
his family mythology was detached
from the reality of his social surroundings

the Rays were so poor
James and his two brothers
(who grew up to be petty criminals as well)
could not even afford the nickel for lunch

but to hear him tell it
he
was the smart one
the ambitious one
the one who would do great things

unusual for a loner

sure
the investigation paints him as a racist
he worked for the George C. Wallace campaign
wrote "Martin Luther Koon"
on the back of the hotel room TV
last time both he and King
were in LA
miles from each other

but being from "Little Dixie" Missouri
the poorest of the poor whites

in a period of economic decline
King was talking about solving poverty
Wallace was talking about blaming somebody

Ray had pride in his race
because that is the only thing he had
to take pride in

assassins are usually in their early twenties
twenty-two, twenty-three
Lee Harvey Oswald was twenty-four
that age where the world is right and wrong
never in between
and they are on fire
with the idea that they can change the world
with a gun and a bullet

seldom are they Ray's age
by forty, the world is more gray
in my professional opinion
he suffered from textbook narcissism
preoccupied with being wanted

I knew he was a fugitive
first time he walked into my office
but unlike most fugitives
he didn't want to be anonymous
he wanted notoriety

four days ago
he was the most wanted man in America

criminal, yes
sociopath, absolutely
killer?

three days ago

my patient pleaded guilty
to the murder of Rev. Martin Luther King Jr.
and today
he says he didn't do it.

Ray:

They still didn't think I could do it
but I showed them
I mean no one had ever done that before, huh

no one has ever escaped Missouri State Penitentiary
but I did

reported to work at the bakery that morning
got into this loading dock box with a fake bottom
they put the bread on top
closed up the box
put me on the truck and rode on out of there

it's NOT an easy place to get away from
maximum security

and *still* didn't make the FBI's most wanted list
I know
I listened everyday
escaped with my Channel Master Transistor Radio

always news
I love news
always this King feller

I love my people
learned how to use fake names
from my parents
skippin' out on bills and mortgages

we moved around a lot
the Law didn't like the Ray family too much
nobody did, really
but we had each other

I remember the winter
we had to break pieces off of our house
for firewood

I talk about memories like these
the time I was doing in Jeff City
with Jerry and John Ray
my brothers, in Chicago
I tell 'em about my escape
and conversations with the Klan
and the brotherhood
and Raul
inside

they talk about kidnapping
pornography
small change

inside?
the word was
$100K for the head of Dr. Martin Luther King

it wasn't about race
it was about money

Black people needing white jobs
poor white people needed relief too
my family!
needed me
to provide
an answer

I was in Canada for a month
before I went to Birmingham, Alabama
bought a Mustang
I saw Wallace
I watched King
I went Puerto Vallarta

I went to LA
saw a few doctors
took dance lessons
became a locksmith
and graduated from bartender school

whole time I stayed in hotels
ate pretty well for a convict
ya know, when you break out of prison
you don't exactly have the time
to stop and get all your personal effects

but I had money coming in
I knew people
people that helped me get what I needed
at least until I figured out how to help my family

then, one day
this King I always see on the TV and the radio
gives me an idea

and the next day
I forward all my mail
general delivery to Atlanta, Georgia
King's hometown

my people are alright about it
so I leave the Wallace campaign and head east
nothing but road, engine, and radio

nothing but King
and his Poor People's March

occupying the National Mall with tents?!
who ever heard of such a thing?

and angry whites
with no jobs and no money
and angry Blacks
with no money and no rights
"redistribution of wealth"
said the newsman on the radio

Edgar Hoover was on the radio
head of the FBI
calling King a big fat liar, front page
and this whole time
I thought he was a minister?

and I get to Atlanta
buy a map and circle King's life
his church
his house
his work
and as I headed back
to wait
I hear him on the radio:

*"I admire the good Samaritan, but I don't want to be one. I don't want to spend
my time picking up people by the side of the road, after they've been robbed and
beaten up. I want to change the Jericho road."*

I knew then
I'd have to meet him in Memphis

see,
he didn't come home
because of one thousand colored sanitation workers
that were on strike in Memphis
wanting higher pay
and union recognition

a detour
news reports said
his staff objected
wanted to focus on Washington
but he said "he must"
"because he promised them"
said he could not ignore the call of his striking brothers

white people were striking too

I loved the news
I arrived in Memphis the same day as King
TV said
that morning
they had to disembark King's plane
of all passengers
pilot said they had to check
for explosives
because King was on board

everybody knew he was coming
they knew what plane
they knew what hotel
they even knew what room number
it was in the news

forty-eight hours later
I *was* the news
I made the news for
buying a gun

I made the news for
buying binoculars

I was in the news for
being alone

I don't know where my people went
I didn't come to Memphis by myself
I came to be part of something
something more powerful than
the stroke of a pen
something more powerful than
a bullet

all I wanted
was to see him for myself
see if he was real

he was

and then he was gone

then they all pointed at me

I don't know how an ex-felon
gets from Memphis
to Detroit
to London

how I don't get caught
'til they decide to catch me

I must've had help
from God or whoever
Percy Foreman, my attorney
advised me to just take a plea

"America is hungry for a hanging
and the Justice Dept. is looking for something to serve."

at least
my story will be worth a fortune
and my family will be taken care of

King was a great man
and my name will forever be mentioned
alongside
in the same breath as his

hadn't seen my news radio
since I fled that rooming house in Memphis
until it was presented to me by the FBI
in the pristine bundle
of all the things they said were mine
as pristine as they found it

but I heard
even in England
that I had finally

finally . . .
made the Most Wanted list.

Hoover:

Also Known As Eric Eschol,
a.k.a. Eric Gault
a.k.a. Harvey Lowmeyer
a.k.a. Ramone Snead
born James Earl Ray

was successfully apprehended
for the killing of Doctor
Martin Luther King

now, I know
my disagreement with King's philosophy
was made public
but I can assure you

we made King our number one priority
put him at the top of our list

we had FBI agents
on the ground
the very next day

pulled every passport issued
after the killing
until we found a match
to Ray's bartending school photograph

we checked Ray's prints
against fifty-three thousand fingerprint cards
of known felons
and we got lucky
on number seven hundred

immediately
upon his capture
in the middle of the night
we flew Ray from London
to Memphis
interrogated him the entire flight
about ties
to an international conspiracy
or a revolutionary faction
to ensure
that he'd be the end of it

but some
will still insinuate

that I had some
mad ten-year obsession
with King
that I
used the power of this office
to destroy his life

nothing
could be further from the truth

we spent
more man hours on the King Manhunt
than any other in history
and in the end
we got our man

I mean
I can appreciate your concern
Doctor Ruffin
but I don't see
what this line of questioning
has anything to do
with our visit today?

BERNICE (A.K.A. FIVE)

I agree.
Daddy was a socialist.

He gave it all,
to everyone. Belonged
to everybody. Didn't save any,
for me.

He made a rotten messiah,
couldn't even save
himself.

When they hung our family a cross
in our front yard,
I thought it was a jungle gym,
until they called him "Jungle"
Jim.

The way it lit
felt like perpetual Christmas Eve.
Like Groundhog Déjà Vu . . .
like tomorrow is never
quite Christmas morning
again. Like Jesus was never born,
again. Like tomorrow is never.

Again. But today adults say the meanest things,
like "Santa is never bringing you
your Daddy back."

When they hung his marriage
on a cross in our front yard,

my mother was on fire.
But she never made a sound.

Neither did I.

Not even when they burned an effigy
of me on the front lawn.
Chanting, "One little girls! One little girls! ..."

Most kids my age
are certain they will live forever,
but my evidence to the contrary
is the empty chair at the head
of the table.

But daddy
was a good sharer,
ask mom.

He gave it up.

So, I gave him up
long before being properly taught
how to share.

He always belonged to them
and God and history books.
Never to me. I belong to
magazine covers and mommy's lap.

To this very day
I still wish I
was the girl of his dreams.

But everyone believed in them.
Everyone believed in him.

Unlike them,
I was unable to believe in Daddy's disappearing act.

Unlike him,
I was unable to believe in things I couldn't see.
But I can do them one better, and LOVE him
instead.

Love him to death.
Even if I cannot make believe he's alive.

My unopened gift
snatched from underneath the King Family Tree,
finally found one morning hung,
on a balcony in Memphis, Tennessee,
like an ornament.

Five is too young to be told
you must share everything you have with the world
because Daddys are dying in Africa
and who the hell do you think you are?

That year, I learned that Christmas
in April is called Easter. That the Holy Book
is predictable. That some people
are born for only one purpose.

I learned "socialist" doesn't mean share,
it means sacrifice.

And that's not fair.

SNOW MOTHS (A.K.A. IF SNOWFLAKES HAD DREAMS . . .)

Sometimes mistaken for butterflies,
but never birds.

Flakes fall the same way,
on this side of the universe . . .

but never mistaken
for falling stars.

SONRISE

In the center of this chest is a solar system
hovering above an empty plexus because
someone left the light on. When the stardust
in these veins burns out, that black hole will find
his way home and thank me for naming him
after a wish. Terrified by the sound of his own vacuum,
and everything else I left behind. Cursing me,
beneath his beating breath, for all this space to fill
and the unnecessary dying of the chakra.

LOVE NOTES

Our relationship
is this piano.

Black-on-black keys
that never flat
nor sharp,
just love notes.

She walks
the baseline
like a tightrope dedication.

Like listening
is an extreme sport.

Like a shout-out
in every smile.

Like she'll give you
her heartbeat boxed
and bowed.

Thank G_d
G_d is a deejay
and she takes requests.

Because our neighbors swear
our headboard resembles
a broken record
a broken record
a broken headboard.

Trying to slow jam our way
into a future of karaoke and karats,
but in the meantime
feelin' them acoustics in the shower . . .

To the rhythm of lips clapping
and windpipes gasping,
salivating for this cell-phone soundtrack,
songs smuggled to one another
in meetings
and eargasms on elevators,
might as well call these hymns and her's "gospel"
the way it saves us.

She's a heartstring Hendrix
and I'm two left hands.
Good thing she likes my delicate fingers.

She asked me if I wanted to be
in her wedding band.
I said I'm more of a Wedding Singer . . .

but I'm no Adam Sandler.

Funny, I can still hear her humming
even when I'm not near her.

Harmonizing lives,
dancing diaphragm-to-diaphragm,
we are a Headstart on one helluva reception,

partnering our pulses
one song
at a time.

STAND: FOR EVERY TEACHER
I EVER HAD OR HADN'T

You stand
Somewhere between
Who they are
And what they could be

Not an obstacle

Quite the contrary
But they can't tell

Their only hint
Is the way you stand

You appear ready to fight
And dammit if sometimes . . .

They do not know it is for them

You are hands down
While they are hands up
In front of you

You take their best shot
And every morrow
Come back for more
Please

You are the space between
The end of every question
And good manners

Between a demand
And a smile

Between please and thank you

Between boredom
And the bathroom

Between bathroom and sh . . .
'tuff we let pass for education in this country

You stand between pass
And fail

Between pass
And learn

Between pass
And future

You stood between Dr. Maya Angelou
And her degree

Her traumatic muteness at eight
And her ability to speak at thirteen

Between Anne Sullivan
And Helen Keller's ability to speak what she sees

You stand between every single student
And their "Story of Me"

Stood with Mary Duncan in Nashville, Tennessee

Between a fourth-grade Oprah Winfrey
And *the* Oprah

And in 1989 you stood on her show
As she said thank you

I thank you

For standing between the spike
And the punch bowl

Between the wallflower
And the wall

Between the two kids
Getting a little too Lambada on the dance floor

Between the blackboard
And the clean slate

Between a paycheck
And a living

Between social promotion
And social skills

Between high-stakes testing
And a high-stakes life

You stand
With a backpack

More camouflage
Than campus

Always at attention
Even in a room full of pupils that lack it

You are a frontline
Of lesson plans waving sayonara from flagpoles
At half mast

You are marching orders
That have accepted
To stand

Between our lil' angels
And the gunmen who have come
To give them wings

Between neck
And bedroom closet

Between bully
And believer

You stand between a sensible workweek
And beyond the call of duty

Between the drugs
And our children's self-esteem

Between banned books
And burnt out

And sometimes . . .
Between the bar
And the weekend you desperately needed

Like two days ago, already!

You are a Monday through Friday
Stand-in parent for *me*
And for every moment you surrogate life
I am away on my knees
Begging for you
And my child
To succeed

For as long
As you've been on your feet for me
I will stand for you.

SIDEWALK SOCIETY

For the City Of Albuquerque Public Art Program 35th Anniversary and Urban Enhancement Trust Fund 30th Anniversary

We are a sidewalk society

now, dead-bolted in
inside four walls of insecurity
lack of community
and lack of street

we were never meant
to be a sit-down society
we were born to be the art
of an elevated heartbeat

we were born to be seen
like the splatter of blood, sweat, and tear
the artist wears on her dungarees
and his sleeves

the things we visit
touch
and touch us

will be forever present in our memory
ever longer than anything
we've only ever seen on a screen

JUST ASK THE ALIENS!

because from a million miles away
Albuquerque's Wikipedia page is text heavy and woefully
underwhelming
so when they welcome themselves to a closer look

Public Art will be the cover of our book

and when Armageddon is at the push of a button
you want every single color inside you on the cover if they're gonna
judge you
when they will annihilate everything that looks the same

if the aliens returned today?

they'd obviously choose here
our state flower is the Aluminum Yucca
and we've been trying to send them Rays of Communication
for more than thirty years

but they no habla New Mex-spañol
and Public Art is the only way to see the shared peace

of our souls

so when we no longer call this space home
these pieces will be the only story told

first, they'll set their sights on the Center of the City
somewhere between the Centennial and 1912
the Solar Arc will mark their radar
and Angelitos de Caridad will act as a lighthouse as well

their Jornada will *actually* find the Cultural Crossroads of the Americas
unlike Oñate
because they will be high technology with a better map
aiming for the globe between Musical Theater Southwest and the Fish
they won't be confused by old and new Route 66,
you can bet your right foot about that

but when they finally land
beneath the Waterfall of the New Moon
under the Nob Hill Gateway

Central lit up like a neon landing strip
they will find us most interesting

first Star past the Taco Bell
the logical place to land
is at Forms Waiting for Word from Other Worlds
and what they find

will remind them of something

how we Bridge Blues
and an Asteroid Sequence 2

the Floating Mesa

our arroyo of light
that turns Bear Canyon into a constellation at night
they would see how trippy it is
to see themselves in our Triptych
and they'd take a trip
but after a few light-years on the road
they'd wanna freshen up

they would observe
the elaborate nature of our signposts
that help rain find river
they will know there was once water here
Milky Starfish smoking gun
it will be obvious by the fossils
evidence left by Spike & Alberta's ancestors
tipped off by Los Altos Skateparkers arcing Mountain Waves
ask the Bird Girl searching for water
if they can borrow her eyeglasses

finally oasis
full sprint into the River of Life to bathe . . .
. . . and *ow!* that hurt!

they will finally find us
a fluidity of life
in their wildest Dreams & Nightmares
at the end of *our* Journey
of Inter & Broken Weaves
finally a Fountain of Peace
and riot

a pool of Alphabet Soup
waterfalling into a puddle of poetry on the plaza
they will finally see us
teach the eyes and touch the spirit

they will finally see us
somewhere between studio and construction
beautifying this ugly
and putting orange cones around the parts of us we want to forget
like César Chávez
when he died with an art book in his fist

they will finally smell us
like dinnertime
and Broadway farmworkers coming in from the field

smell us like an airplane
coming out of the armpit of what they call
"The Lady Liberty of Meso-America"
at the McDonald's across from the McDonald's
at Yale University's UNM Park
at University of New Mexico's Yale Park

they will finally hear this
Living Memorial
because we are nothing more than family lines in this linear park
raised a barely teenage mural

on the Convention Center wall
Matachines & Malinche
purity and everything that is beautiful in this world
we've solemnly sworn
to make our city a landmark

they will do more than finally find us
they cannot miss us, here
where the porcupine moon
rises and sets itself on the West Mesa

they will be Cruising San Mateo
once,
twice,
three times an alien

disturbed
at the new ice age or climate catastrophe
that petrified the Hummingbird, Toad, and Dragonfly . . .

and, particularly, the Coyote with the Woman Inside

pleasantly surprised
that the cats have evolved to three-piece suits
and polite conversation on park benches

familiar,
with the Giant Red Snake
and the life-sized video game in front of Cibola High
that reminds them of cousins and house pets,
respectively

giddy,
at the site of an Elvis Impersonator
and the ribbon in the sky at the Sunport

because radio waves only get longer in a vacuum
and the King and Stevie
been bouncing back and forth off black holes since
the Big Band

and in the end

they will check the Bird of Time Sundial,
cause Daylight Savings doesn't exactly "do it" for the rest of the
universe

jack the Positive Energy of New Mexico sculpture
that is a perfect fit for the broken Fahrvergnügen on their ship
hard to find a mechanic that works on exports in this part of the galaxy,
if ya know what I mean?

and they will turn the Tri-centennial towers into a slingshot
In order to David and Goliath their spacecraft outta here . . .

Leaving our legacy intact for future incarnations . . .

Well,
minus Tony Dellaflora,
Don Quixote's Suitcase
and a piece of Elizabeth Naranjo Pottery that they took as "souvenirs"

Only,
photographic memory of Presbyterian and Catholic churches
Madonna of the Trail and Guadalupe
as holy sisters of facial recognition

dreams of Water and the Memory of Sky Bear

they will leave us alone
in our backbreaking pursuit to Heal our Garden

with a talking Mona Lisa of Gordon Church
reminding Albuquerque
to speak for herself
define her "identity
beyond constructing streets, buildings, and parks."

LAW ENFORCEMENT OATH OF HONOR

Raise your right hand,
and repeat after me ...
I do solemnly declare
upon my honor and conscience
that I will act, at all times,
to the best of my ability and knowledge
in a manner befitting a police officer.

I do,
take this community to be my lawfully
wedded life.
To have and hold,
in sickness and in health
'til death do us in.

I do solemnly swear,
with my hand on this bible
instead of this rifle,
in this court of public opinion,
that I am not judge
nor jury
nor Jesus.

I am just
a servant,
sworn to protect
this community.
I do thee serve.
I will preserve
the dignity
and will respect the rights
of all individuals.

I will reserve
the right to respect the dignity
of all individuals.

I will serve,
to the best of my dignity,
respect for all.
I will discharge my duties
with integrity
and will promote understanding
and conciliation.

I will discharge
only when it is my duty,
only when we're beyond understanding,
only when we are beyond conciliation.
I will *only* discharge integrity.
I will *not* discharge.
Not even when my life is threatened.
Only when your life is in danger,
because I signed up to be a hero
not a coward.

Because the greatest thing I should be afraid of
is losing my community's trust.
Because anyone can get a gun
and call themselves a cowboy,
but not every gun can get a conscience
and call himself a cop.

I will exercise my authority
as a police officer

in the manner intended by the law.
I will exercise my compassion
as a police officer
because I am not above the law,
because it is not beneath me,
because I am not "the law,"
just another one of the people
the law protects.

I will faithfully obey
the orders of my superiors,
and will be ready
to confront danger
in the line of duty.
It is my duty
To faithfully obey
my moral compass,

and will be ready
to confront my superiors
when they are out of line.
And that's an order!

I will act with honesty,
courtesy, and regard
for the welfare of others,
and will endeavor to develop
the esprit de corps.

I will not act.
I will *be* honesty, personified.
I will *be* courtesy of personhood
even to those without homes
or on welfare.

I will endeavor to say
"Hello" from time to time.

Develop morale in the community
because it's bigger than some code,
because it's bluer than some code,
and desperately in need of sunlight.
Because the root word of morale
is moral.

And because it's just as easy
to always be looking for
what someone has done right
as it is to always be looking for
what someone is doing wrong.

I solemnly swear
to be as obsessed with building community
as I am with broken laws.
I will act justly
and impartially
and with propriety
toward my fellow officers.
So long as they are just,
impartial,
and proper
toward my fellow citizens.

I do solemnly declare
upon my honor and conscience
that I *will* act
like an officer of the peace
at all times,
to the best of my ability and knowledge.
I will constantly strive to honor
this oath in my service
as a police officer,
so help me God.

A.A. (AFRO-ANONYMOUS, A.K.A. "IN RECOVERY," A.K.A. WARDROBE)

> I am an invisible man. . . . I am a man of substance, of flesh and bone,
> fiber and liquids—and I might even be said to possess a mind. I am
> invisible, understand, simply because people refuse to see me.
>
> —RALPH ELLISON, *Invisible Man*

Son, if you came up missing
your hood would not be able to find you.
Unable to pick you out in a crowd,
or a police lineup.

If you made it that far.
If they even came looking at all.

Don't be anonymous, child.
Make sure you stick out
like a pair of sore thumbs
alongside eight other fingers.
Don't fist.
Don't flinch,
even when their fingers
curl horizontally at your chest.

They won't pull if you don't push,
I pray.

Get 'em up, high.
As though you could actually reach
those pruned dreams above you,
rotting on each and every branch of government.

Like you're the one being robbed of something,
and everything is suspect.

When standing up for yourself
becomes a crime,
you better stand out.

Like flannel in the summertime.
Like black combat boots and a trench coat
any time of year.
Like Steven Fuckin' Urkel,
pants 'round your nipples,

or they will put shackles around your ankles.
Hoodies around your neck.
Flowers around your casket.

Because they murder more Stephons
than Steves every single year.

Don't be anonymous, son.
Even if your comrades wear fatigues
every day in this war zone
and call it a wardrobe,
you rock those plaid shorts
like a Tiger with no stripes.
Do not enlist in Mortal Kombat
with a metropolitan military
that can't see the fathers for the Gs,
our future for the tress.

It is open season on hoodies
and skinny jeans.
The only bulletproof vest
I can offer you is beneath
this three-piece suit.

We've worn these neckties for years
because we're least threatening
at the end of a leash.

Speak jive only
as a second language,
because when in Rome
do as conquered people do.

I know . . .
Romans who?
Empires aren't covered
'til long after first grade,
but it's never too soon to grow up
in this backward world
of men in backward hats
getting gunned down in Walmart
for brandishing a toy pistol.

While manufacturers live to brand
another day, about how lifelike
their product is . . .

"So authentic,
even cops can't tell the difference . . ."

So anonymous,
even cops can't tell the difference.

Son,
this is not cops and robbers,
this is cowboys and Indians,
and the only way to not get shot in the back
is to dress like a cowboy.

This poem
is the only arrow pointing you past nineteen.

When their life
or pride
is in danger,
they cannot tell the difference between you
and the criminal record
they been bumping in their patrol car all day.

The gangsta rap videos
they imagine on loop in your brain
every time you open your mouth
with no "sir."

They can't tell,
just like mothers
trying to identify the mutilated bodies
of their babies.

Pulling Stephon's
personal effects
out of a footlocker
of Air Force Ones
and Phoenix Suns jerseys
like it's a police lineup.

I will donate
your carefully creased curb costume
to a "Pimps and Hoes" party
at a fraternity you will never get in
at a college I am determined to get you into
. . . in one piece.

This retired uniform,
designed to help you survive
these gang-infested streets,
is in need of a facelift
to help you survive
a more lethal form of thuggery.

Because your tank tops
will never top their tanks.
If wearing a white flag were enough
I would drape you in that,
but it looks too much like the coroner's blanket,
and Officer PTSD might mistake you
for a frontline in Iraq.

Take off that bull's-eye of conformity, son.
That bullshit dream of equality.
You can't wear whatever you want in this country
that blames women for their own rape
because of what they didn't have on.

You tuck your blackness into your bloodstream
like a white gold chain in the most dangerous part of town,
because the bullets pierce bubble goose parkas,
leaving puddles of black boyhood flooding our sewers.

And I'm sorry,
but I'd rather have you crying
than leaking
on your way home.

So you will settle
for being the preppiest kid in school.
Wear your culture
like a butt-naked emperor.

Like an invisible man.

They will see you when it's convenient,
beyond your Birkenstocks and Brooks Brothers,
during the next manhunt.
When boys are fair game.

So, whatever you do,
don't be anonymous.

When you go back out to that corner
be the duck wearing a Labrador Retriever costume
in a flock of geese.

At least you know
they won't shoot you, today.
And hey,
if you are lucky,
they might even housebreak you,
and take you home.

DIAL UP

I put two thousand miles between us
in 2005,

between him and his first grandson in 2007.
The only time he ever set foot in Albuquerque . . .

Between him and my career.
He heard me read long poems aloud in Camden once.
In West Chester, days after we lost Grandpa,

in 2005.

But in the latter days,
he only heard me preach at weddings
and funerals . . .

the shortest poem I ever shared at one of those
was the one he couldn't hear

at his.

In the latter years,
as his brain started deleting itself,
he started repeating himself.

I love you. I love you. I love you.
But it wasn't a glitch.

Why are you so far from home?
. . . was my malfunction.

I haven't been home in eight months now.
Pre-pandemic I flew home four to six times

a year.

I wish we were closer,
now more than ever.

I wish for all those times I laid in bed with him,
the Sundays I kept him company

while Mom went to go pastor his flock,
when I read him my poetry

instead of the paper.

All those times he held full-on conversations
with ghosts, and I held

his hands.

I wish he could hold my hand today.
And even though *he's* the one,
now light-years away

. . . I hope he stays in touch.

CORONA

But if a woman have long hair, it is a glory to her: for her hair is
given her for a covering. But if any man seem to be contentious,
we have no such custom, neither the churches of God.

—I CORINTHIANS 15–16

Either way
it is your birthright,

whether matrilocal
or matrilineal.
By gender.
By God.

Manifest destiny claims your kingdom
and acts like we are doing you "a solid"
by calling you queen.

By calling that "a crown"
without understanding the proper rules of engagements.

That Sundays aren't *just* the Lord's Day.
It was a feather in the cap of the slave,
the couple dollars you could squeeze out of being overworked
and underpaid to bless yo'self to something nice,
to the only place you could afford to wear it, no cover.
Sunday is also the Pageant of Christ.

1. Don't wear a hat wider than your shoulders.
2. Don't wear a hat that is darker than your shoes.
3. If your hat has feathers, make sure they are never bent nor broken.
4. No sequins in the daytime.

5. No borrowing under absolutely any circumstances
(if you give it, YOU GIVE IT! as an heirloom, as a gift).

6. You should never look lost in it.
7. Attitude. You have to have one in order to wear a hat well, dahling.
8. Easter hats should be white, cream, or pastel—even if it's still cold outside.
9. When they sacrifice your son, find one as big as his smile

to wear to his funeral.

Keep them in boxes too.
A brand-new one for every such occasion,
Mother's Days and Resurrection Sundays included.
Sadly and gladly
by the time you are a grandmother
you will have enough to go around . . .

as reminders.

Remember, veils render them convertible, all purpose,
any occasion, just like Big Mama's little black dress.

As you recount the parable of Jesus washing the disciples' feet,
I learn from watching you
to interpret that as
God never wanting me to set foot in a church without looking *clean*.

A sign of prosperity
because in the hood *and* the holla
God smiles upon our people in church hats and sneaker heads.

But I refuse to call that "a crown,"
because you are not who you are
simply because of who you married.

Because man confers kings and queens, not God.
God's in the business of putting wings on the backs of moms.

I prefer to think of it as a halo,
because unlike a crown
it never comes off,
not even when you are at work
bussing beer bottles on the night shift.

Because Monday through Saturday you are a walking miracle.

But on Sundays
you are a walking museum.

OPEN EMAIL . . . TO THE FUTURE

written for the National Conference for Media Reform, 2013

do you remember us?

before I wrote you letters like this
in cursive
and you told me
I was not your type

before b4
when your word
had vowels
and we
had promise
and should've kept both

when we were still stories

like the one Reverend Vivian still tells
about the preachers and their protest
the time we turned that jail cell
into a low-power FM
turned us into a one-hit wonder
and those ministers sang us over and over again
even after they were told to shut up

otra vez

even after they were told they'd lose their mattresses

otra vez

even after they were mattress-less

they sang us again
do you remember when
we spelled "I love you"
with ten songs, a cassette, a piece of tape
and a sharpie

wrote "possible wedding songs" on it
scratched that
and wrote "I like you a lot vol. 1"

and he gave it to her
and she gave one to her
and he gave one to him
and they all had the same ten songs on it

back when we thought
the digital revolution meant five finger
instead of fist

back when music "gigs"
meant something different
back when we couldn't fit a library of songs in our pocket
but we could in our heart

back when we
actually had to remember phone numbers
and stop and ask for directions

instead of bitching at google maps
and still having to stop and ask for directions

back when we had to admit
that we were lost
that we didn't know it all

you remember

when it was
the satanic static
in the wax
that charmed daddy into drunk dancing
instead of damage

when we used to cozy up
to the snap, crackle, pop
of the radio just to keep warm

when the walls between family members
started wearing moving pictures
to give the illusion of spending time together

remember when knowing what buttons
not to push prevented distance and silence
and now it just prevents silence

when weeknight meant
gather round the table for
TV dinner with TV parents
and grace went like this
"at least we're not hungry & orphaned"
thank God for the Huxtables
and both mom's jobs

when Neil Armstrong landed on the boob
when the Challenger moonwalked and moonwalked and
moonwalked
on instant replay

when space stations started beaming
stardust to our rooftops
to remind us that *we*
are radiant

when gamma rays only meant one thing
and it was not catching cancer from your cell phone
just like Lou Ferrigno
forever worried about how big
when we should've been worried about how green

remember when super bowl commercials didn't suck

when one bully was enough
but her smartphone is more socially awkward than her
so she keeps a gang in her pocket
that pummels her where it won't leave bruises
until it mega hurts

this email will self-destruct
if the colonizers keep trying to plantation the Internet

the airwaves are no place for a slave ship
the people think they are free
when they are the cash crop

remember when we said we would
railroad this superhighway under the ground
before we let them take us
Pandora an old negro spiritual station
to pirate information
with Dr. King broomsticking morse code
underneath the beat when it's his turn to speak

remember that we
are the first amendment
the only industry protected by law
the lifeblood of the republic
protecting democracy
since long before Ben Franklin went postmaster general

how could you forget
our endangered languages?
native tongue severed
newspaper noosed . . .
since the telephone is extinct
I wrote you this by hand
worth more to you now as a collector's item
quaint as a stamp
before postage cost an arm
and a laptop

you can't forget

the names of dead homies
haunt the address book on your phone
their Facebook page a shrine

re-live Newtown in pictures on a screen
and call it therapy
so you don't have to re-live flashes in your mind
and call it PTSD

I wish I was still a piece of paper
not this immortal
this god
corporations are trying to bottle and make a wish

than at least I could be burned
and people would tether together around me again
hands held

the light I'd produce
would be warm, not blue
but temporary

and they'd read each other's face
for real
for once
for ever

and then
they'd sing

ABQ MANIFESTO

For We Are This City

We be
a bucket of Rio,
two handfuls of mesa,
an open box full of God
between the Sandias
and the volcanoes
our name is mud.

We be
close enough to heaven
and clear enough of sky
for the creator
to mouth-to-mouth us alive.

We make dirty
the new "immaculate,"
make car washes obsolete.

We be
urban farmhands
for rural app developers,
be the best brewed beans
and microbrew
in a six-mesa radius . . .

in a hundred mañana radius.

We be coffee shop crushes
and conversations.

We be the creme de la creatives.
We powder with pollen
and monsoon foundation for makeup,
on the rare occasion we "make up,"
only when the winter white tablecloths the mesa.

We be aquifers
of brown gold.
We be the same colored souls.

We be an open-heart horizon.
Transplants, land grants,
and colonial survivors.

We be
people of the earth
and out of this world

at the same time.
We inherit this pride.
This "keep it real" estate of intellectual property.

We B-Q-U-E-R-Q-U-E, aye!

We be
sunsets so beautiful
they paint themselves
on the edge of the earth.

We be
where dreams come to live
and retire.

We be
artists making careers
out of thin air.

We be
made-up words like
"Sunport."

Because stars gotta land somewhere?
Because the center of the universe
has gotta be somewhere?
Because even "the sun"
has a vacation home in New Mexico.
Because we be made upwards
not down words
like mountaintop, we be

adobe inside and out.
We might look like
armored vegetarians, but on the inside
we be the coolest *gatas* you'll ever meet.

We be
entrepreneurs and doers.
Somewhere between bright ideas and
"done and done."

We be
chile by blood and balloon for lungs.

We be
no "I" in team, but two in familia.

We be
full moons and photosynthesis,
not a cloud to be found.

We be radiant.
Worshipping the skies
with hand signs that 5-oh-5
to remind our unidentified flying cousins
that we out here,

fighting for our light.

We be loco.
We be local.
We be lobos
singing to the night.

We are your favorite city's
favorite city.

The heart of the Southwest
leaning just a li'l to the left
in New Mexico's chest.

JANUARY 19, 2017

Dear President Obama,

I would like to offer a poem. A sentiment that hopefully speaks to the singularity of existence that you've so gracefully endured over the past eight years. A unicorn among both presidents and Black people. I imagine it must get lonely. I hope this relates.

The last time they burned the White House was during the War of 1812. The same evening First Lady Dolley Madison planned an extravagant dinner party to which no one came because the British were coming. James Madison would not make it back in time to rendezvous with her, so in order to spare her life the plan was for her to flee. Out the back door of the White House, alone with her slave. Reckless abandon. You were unheard of, descendant of the employee entrance and exit. First president in history to have ever worn a wave cap. So they fingerprint you guilty of making waves. In the very next sentence call you centrist. Slang for Middle Passage. So, you Ivory Coasted into office, with an overwhelming three-fifth of the electoral college. It is ironic that your nickname isn't landslide. Instead it is the skin of your teeth that makes you George Washington of Black America. That makes this White House unlivable after you.

The third term is when they box you up and send your Black ass back to Chicago. Home, with a care package of all the paintings that spook you. Put them on your wall as a reminder of the second-floor residence. Your sanctuary. No Secret Service. The only place in the world that your family can be Black in peace. The most powerful man in the world constantly followed. Every step. Every store. Ever after. Except for these couple thousand feet of dream . . . But as you descend the Grand Staircase for the last time like Moses from Pisgah Peak, like King from the second floor of the Lorraine, bags and family in tow, you recount the moment you were first brought to the orangery. When they showed you Andrew Jackson's Magnolia, pointed to a limb with your name on it, and suggested you plant a tree for Sasha and Malia too.

You recount the public picnics that used to be held daily on the South Lawn up until Grover Cleveland and wish they were called something else. You recount that there was not a bigger house in the nation than this home you now vacate until Civil War South erected mansions to remind this country that there is nothing more powerful than our right to plantation. You recall all the things they called you, all the times they tried to recount and recall you. And on the way out, you are reminded that the last time a nigger was welcome to dine in the White House, as the president's equal, was 1901. Teddy Roosevelt (a progressive Republican) broke bread with Booker T. Washington. After which, another Black would not taste the White House for twenty-eight years. And between now and then, you convince yourself that it is both legacy and policy to burn every president's bed linens upon leaving.

—Hakim

LAST DAY, FIRST DAY (REVISITED)

Evening After

I cried a few times today. When my Poet Laureate successor Jessica
Helen Lopez read her amazing acceptance remarks, when Valerie
Martinez thanked me on behalf of our beautiful city, when I saw
Jessica's beautiful family take the group photo with her . . . I was
reminded of my installation ceremony with the mayor and the poetry
community, but not my son or family there . . . and it made me sad . .
. because the most important people should love the most important
things you do (besides loving them, of course). And I missed my
son today, but at least I get to share the stage with him tonight, and
tomorrow, and many years to come. But I smiled and laughed a lot
today too, Burque. Because you've made me feel important and loved
when I needed it most . . . and in many ways you saved me. You made
poetry my job. You always showed up, and all I did was try to return the
favor as much as possible. I am eternally grateful for the opportunity to
serve you. Muchimas gracias. I love you. Private Bellamy, signing off.
#OverAndOut

Morning After (First Day)

What did I do the day after the laureateship? Same thing I did the
morning after I was given it. Same thing I do before and after every
impossible moment of my career: pray and run faster. I went for a long
run downtown . . . to survey the beauty of what I'd be responsible for
representing. To breathe the air . . . and on this beautiful morning, I
went to breathe . . . again. Good morning, Albuquerque. I feel like I
haven't seen you in two years. ;) #YouAreStillGorgeous

MAYOR

for Richard J. Berry

It's premature
to call the race
a "race."

When in fact
the election
is just the beginning.

After all the stripes,
lanes, names & numbers
you are left both podium
and custodian.

With expectations
that you run again . . .

That the times go down,
even as your age inches up.

That you fasten your accomplishments
and do more
          in less.

All while tending to the track,
making sure both the idling
and passing lanes are open
to fast and slow alike.

Being mayor
is like going from the Olympics
to Parks & Rec,

and it's funny.

There's no way
to practice
for this competition.

Only on-the-job training,
an exercise in endurance.
Both long haul
and quick study.

Because it is more
than being fit to serve;
it is live and learn.

It is finishing
what you started,
and every stride in between.

From the farmers' market
to the press conferences,
the Panda Bear christenings
and the fallen officers.

There is a pedometer
in your pocket
that serves as evidence
of the time you've spent
on your feet
for your team,

Albuquerque.

And as you ride off into the stands,
sunset in hand . . .
you suddenly realize
the resemblance between a diploma
and a baton.

That's why students
make the best coaches,
                    pass it on.

Because long before we raise any banners,
our job is to take care
of our bodies.

And at this
municipal track meet,
every body
means the well-being
of our *entire* team.

Belonging to each other
is the real race,
because we never run
alone . . .

we just take turns.

There's a marathon
in every lesson,
but the hurdles

are free.

CITY OATH

. . . on the Inauguration of Mayor Tim Keller

If more politicians knew poetry, and more poets knew politics, I
am convinced the world would be a little better place in which to
live.

—JOHN F. KENNEDY

What if
we elected one another
instead of someone

somewhere else?

And I mean "each other,"
elect to belong
      to something

that is bigger
than what sets us apart.

What if we elected to belong
to *all* our problems
and *all* the solutions?

The problems
we may or may not have started.

The ones
we pretend to have nothing to do with.

What if we woke up every morning
being choosey?

What if the only thing we abandoned
was entrapment
rather than our duties?

Because I, for one,
have had a "love/plate" relationship with this town,
and between these four walls
(and my relationship counselor)
I learned that if I treat
every single morning I awake
this side of the Rio Grande

as though Albuquerque's choosing me . . .
and vice versa . . .

it's easier to find common ground
somewhere between the Valley
and the Heights, to see
what's working.

To dream bigger than what isn't.
To do better than
if it ain't broke, don't fix it.

Because good government
is sorta like running a business,
the business of bringing the impossible
into existence.

The things we cannot do alone, together.

Like moving the private sector
toward public interest.

Because "the public"
is wholly made up of private citizens.

Like people before party
and politics,
sorta like the Golden Rule
long before organized religion.

Because even the Bible says
that church is just a building,
and the real temple
is found within the people in it.

And government is similar:
wherever two or more are gathered
on a mission
underneath these double rainbows
serves as a covenant between community members.

Because a city where everyone is afraid of each other
can't be good for our children,
much less tourism.

So every four years or so
we treat ourselves to an intervention;
to assess whether we are still addicted to our problems
we roll out a parade of ideas and good intentions

and call it an election.

Recommit to the oneness
of one another
'til we 'part
for the poles again.

Pledging city
over self,
reminded
that *this* city
is just

a ristra of selves
bound by tierra
and time.

In a place
of shared responsibility,
where regardless
of who we did
or *didn't* vote for,

we are all mayor
should we choose to accept it.

Pledging anything we want . . .

especially if it's wanting
to wake up here.

NOTES

The following poems were composed as original commissions: "One Hundred Years of Corridos: A Song for the New Mexico Centennial," "ABQ Manifesto," "Bernice (a.k.a. Five)," "Blue Corn Special," "Bread & Roses," "Corona," "Doc: A Monologue Tryptych," "Fisher Price School of Medicine," "For 'Nikki,'" "Law Enforcement Oath of Honor," "New Mexico Department of Tourism (A Haiku)," "Open Email . . . to the Future," "Sidewalk Society," and "Stand: For Every Teacher I Ever Had or Hadn't."

The following poems were composed during the author's tenure as Albuquerque Poet Laureate (2012–2014): "One Hundred Years of Corridos: A Song for the New Mexico Centennial," "Bless Me," "Blue Corn Special," "Bread & Roses," "Doc: A Monologue Tryptych," "Fisher Price School of Medicine," "For 'Nikki,'" "Law Enforcement Oath of Honor," "New Mexico Department of Tourism (A Haiku)," Open Email . . . to the Future," "Sidewalk Society," and "Stand: For Every Teacher I Ever Had or Hadn't."

"January 19, 2017" and "Last Day, First Day (Revisited)" were first published in Erik Benjamins, *Last Day, First Day* (Los Angeles: No Style Press, 2017).

"Bread & Roses" was first published by *World Literature Today* (November 2013).
"A.A. (Afro-Anonymous, a.k.a. "In Recovery," a.k.a. WARdrobe)" was first published by *Alternet* (April 2014) and subsequently published in *Understanding & Dismantling Privilege Journal* (December 2015).

CREDITS

"One Hundred Years of Corridos: A Song for the New Mexico Centennial": © Hakim Bellamy, June 12, 2012

"Fisher Price School of Medicine": © Hakim Bellamy, November 3, 2014

"Bless Me": © Hakim Bellamy, October 29, 2012

"Bread & Roses": © Hakim Bellamy, New Mexico Federation of Labor Annual Conference 2012

"Blue Corn Special": © Hakim Bellamy, October 2nd, 2013, for Fuze Southwest 2013

"For 'Nikki'": This poem was written by the Poet Laureate of Albuquerque as a "welcome" to Dr. Nikki Giovanni when she visited Albuquerque, New Mexico, on November 2, 2013.

"Doc: A Monologue Tryptych": This poem was written for and delivered to the students of Amy Biehl High School on January 16, 2012, in honor of their service during Martin Luther King Jr. ; Day.

"Bernice (a.k.a. Five)": Bernice Albertine King (born March 28, 1963) is an American minister and the youngest child of civil rights leaders Martin Luther King Jr. and Coretta Scott King. She was five years old when her father was assassinated (Wikipedia).

"Stand: For Every Teacher I Ever Had or Hadn't": © Hakim Bellamy December 31, 2012

"Sidewalk Society": © Hakim Bellamy October 7, 2013

"Law Enforcement Oath of Honor": © Hakim Bellamy, April 13, 2014

"A.A. (Afro-Anonymous, a.k.a. "In Recovery," a.k.a. WARdrobe)": © Hakim Bellamy, August 15, 2014

"Corona": © Hakim Bellamy, May 13, 2017

"Open Email . . . to the Future": © Hakim Bellamy, April 5, 2013

Printed in the USA
CPSIA information can be obtained
at www.ICGtesting.com
LVHW010555101023
760663LV00003B/254

9 780826 363176